How to Shine a Shoe

HOW TO

SHINE A SHOE

*A Gentleman's Guide to
Choosing, Wearing, and Caring
for Top-Shelf Styles*

•

Written by **STEVE DOOL**

Illustrations by
BILL BRAGG *and*
TOBATRON

Clarkson Potter/Publishers
NEW YORK

CONTENTS

You've probably heard people say that shoes make the man.

Of course, if taken literally, this sentiment is genuinely crazy. Plenty of amazing people have terrible shoes, and vice versa. But still . . . there is something there worth considering. Your shoes won't make you a man, for sure, but they may reveal a little bit more about you than you might initially expect. It would be a leap to say you should trust someone in a pair of well-maintained derbies more than someone in a pair that hasn't been polished since they were purchased. But it's not totally out of bounds to conclude that one man pays more attention to detail than another. Or that one man takes greater pride in his appearance, or maybe even possesses a bit more worldliness or sophistication or just some unmistakably good taste.

Above all that, though, wearing shoes that are well made and appropriate for the occasion allows your personality and natural smarts to shine through, free from the distraction that unfortunate footwear can provide. And, ultimately, that's all you can ask for: not that better shoes make you a better person, but that they allow you the room to demonstrate what makes you *you*.

To that end, this book is designed to give you all the basics you need to make an educated decision when it comes to your next shoe purchase, and the steps beyond: cleaning, maintenance, what to wear where, and how to wear them. In these pages, you'll find some rules of thumb to live by, and some rules that you can (and should) feel free to break. This is about taking it all in and figuring out what works best for you.

So step right in. Learn about Goodyear welt construction and what makes an oxford an oxford, when to take your shoes to a cobbler and why Italian leather is so well regarded. You'll ensure that any assumptions people make about you are at least reflective of your informed decisions. And you can walk in confidence knowing that if somebody is making assumptions about you, it's not because of your footwear.

So, no, your shoes are never going to make you, but at least now you can be sure they won't break you, either.

Enjoy and good luck, gents.

Chapter One

THE
FUNDAMENTALS

HOW TO SHINE A SHOE

To a certain extent, it's possible to identify a quality pair of shoes without knowing what went into making them, in the same way you can tell a decent glass of wine from a $4.99 bottle without knowing a thing about top notes and terroir. A lot of the work is done by trusting your intuition and applying a little common sense. But understanding the name and function of each component that forms your footwear is key to appreciating the craftsmanship that goes into each pair. How a shoe is made—and, specifically, how well it's made—is often the most important differentiating factor that justifies its price at retail and, therefore, informs smart buying decisions. After all, you would be more willing to spend more money on a pair of shoes that is built to last, right?

You already probably know the basics of footwear fundamentals: the tongue, the sole, eyelets, the heel. In some cases, there isn't much more than that, and, depending on the style of shoe in question, there may be even less. To that end, let's discuss a list of different footwear parts, from topline to nitty-gritty.

ANATOMY OF A SHOE

*Here are all the basic parts
you need to know.*

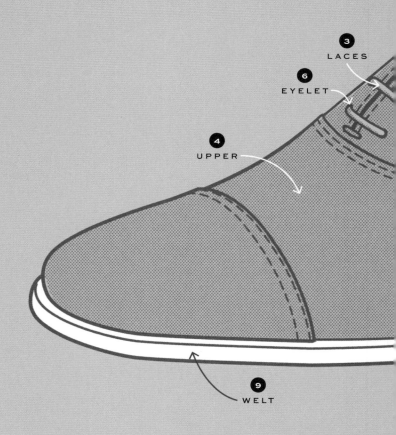

3 LACES

6 EYELET

4 UPPER

9 WELT

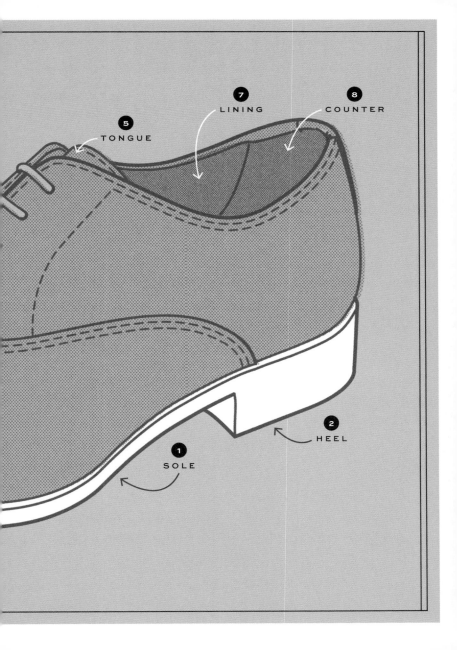

SOLE

The sole is, yes, the bottom portion of your shoe. It's the foundation, if you will, and is often the part that bears the brunt of the wear and tear, since it makes contact with the street, or, if your date is so lucky, the dance floor. On sneakers, the sole is almost always rubber, but for shoes, it's common to find it crafted from leather, which is traditionally considered more formal. Typically, a leather sole is made from layers of the material; as you would assume, the more layers, the more durable the shoe is, generally speaking. If you want to break it down further, the portion of the sole that makes contact with your foot is called the insole, and the portion that makes contact with the outside world is the outsole.

....

HEEL

The back portion of the shoe, attached to the sole on the underside, is called the heel. It can be crafted from stacked pieces of leather or from rubber, and it largely determines how much added height the shoe gives the wearer. The front of the heel is sometimes called the breast. If there is another piece of material attached to the heel, over where it would otherwise connect with the ground, that is called a top piece.

....

LACES

As long as they match the color of the shoe, why should laces even matter? Well, you do actually have some options to consider beyond that. Most formal shoelaces are made from cotton that has been coated in wax for extra durability. They can be rounded or flat—if forced to choose, rounded laces are a safe bet. If you do opt for flat, keep them thin; fat and flat might end up looking too casual, like sneaker laces. Also, check the length. If the laces are too long when tied, you'll end up stepping on them. Thirty-one-inch laces should put you in a good place.

④ UPPER

The upper is, as the name suggests, the part of the shoe above the welt or sole. Essentially, it's what covers the top and sides of your foot. It can be broken down in several different sections:

- *the vamp:* the front to middle section of the upper
- *the quarter:* the back portion of the upper
- *the heel cup:* in some cases, there is an additional patch of material sewn to the front or back of the shoe, which can be decorative or designed to strengthen those sections
- *toe cap:* the front of the upper, which is not to be confused with the toe box, the name for the shape the front of the shoe takes

⑤ TONGUE

You know where the tongue is, but do you know why it's there? Primarily, it's a gentle barrier that provides your foot with extra comfort against the friction of the laces. It also makes it easier to put the shoe on.

⑥ EYELET

These holes through which laces are woven are sometimes reinforced with other, stiffer material to keep them from stretching. The portion of the shoe with eyelets is often called the facing, and it always sits over the tongue. The way the facing is attached determines whether the shoe is called closed-laced or open-laced. Typically, closed-laced shoes are considered more formal than open-laced shoes, but you can decide which you like better based on your own personal taste when we discuss the different types of shoes in the next chapter. From a construction point of view, just know that in closed-laced shoes, the facing is sewn underneath the vamp, giving it a streamlined feel. Open-laced shoes, then, are sewn on top of the vamp, so that they allow for—you guessed it—an opening at the bottom, lending the shoe a more rugged look.

....

LINING

Lining is a catch-all term for the interior material of any given shoe. Some shoes have additional padded lining or fabric lining or may even take the technology used in sneakers to make it feel as though you're wearing a pair of tennis shoes (a secret only you need to know).

....

COUNTER

You can think of the counter as serving the same function as the heel cup, but it exists inside the shoe, typically between the upper and the lining. It's there for added support.

WELT

The welt connects the sole of the shoe to the rest of it (which is called the upper—we'll get to that next). For dress shoes, it's usually also made from leather and frequently stitched on in a process referred to as Goodyear welt construction. That method is named after Charles Goodyear Jr., the man who invented the machine that's used to do the stitching. Other processes bypass a welt, stitching the sole directly to the upper by hand, for example (often called Blake stitch construction). Some shoes, often less expensive pairs, don't incorporate stitching to a welt at all, with soles bonded to the upper using an adhesive or nails.

Put Your Money Where Your Welt Is

If you're going to be putting your shoes through a lot of daily use, pay attention to the construction of the sole and the welt before you make a purchase, to make sure you'll be able to extend the shoes' life for as long as possible. "Goodyear-welted shoes can be resoled up to three times if necessary, making them good value for the money," notes Dan Rookwood, the U.S. editor for the online men's retailer Mr Porter. Soles that have been bonded to the upper using an adhesive may not withstand rigorous use quite as well.

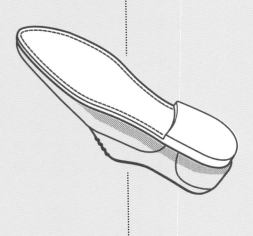

GAUGE THE QUALITY OF LEATHER SHOES

In the world of dress shoes, leather is king. But not all leather is created equal. Here is a handy guide to some common types of leather to help you make sense of it all. And in case you're wondering, there is no one source from which to obtain shoe leather—cattle hide is still the most common, but you can also find leather shoes made from the skins of crocodiles, deer, buffalo, stingrays, and more. If that makes you squeamish or if you're morally opposed to wearing animal hides, vegan-leather shoes crafted from synthetic materials are an easy-to-find, certified cruelty-free alternative (see page 19).

Today, many shoemakers experiment with using different types of leathers on different shoes, throwing a lot of the tried-and-true rules out the window. If you'd like to stick to the basics, the more smooth and shiny the leather is (such as patent leather), the more formal it will look. The inverse is also true; rough-hewn leather with visible imperfections (such as full-grain leather) makes shoes look more casual.

But that doesn't help you identify cheap leather from the real-deal quality variety. For that, here are some key things to look out for:

CONSIDER THE PRICE

It's unfortunate but often true: Leather is expensive. If you see a pair of shoes on sale for considerably less money than others, poor-quality leather could be one reason why.

USE YOUR SENSES

Touch, smell, and look closely at the leather. Leather generally requires breaking in, but it shouldn't be stiff as a board or super-flimsy, either. You want a material that feels like it can handle some wear and tear but still have a bit of movement to it. If you can see points where leather is cracking or if the edges are ragged, it could be a sign the shoemaker likes to cut corners. And if it's supposed to be leather but it doesn't have that leather smell, it's probably not good (and it might not even be the real thing).

EXAMINE THE SHOE AS A WHOLE

This is not a foolproof metric, but looking at the rest of the shoe can offer some hints, too, following the general logic that shoemakers who have invested in pricey leather will also want to surround it with other quality materials and use careful construction to bind it all together. Does the sole feel sturdy? Does the stitching look uniform and tight? Are the laces coated evenly and cleanly? If not, it could be cause for concern.

LEATHER GLOSSARY

GRAIN

The technical term for any texture or imperfections a given piece of leather may have on its exterior

FULL-GRAIN LEATHER

From the topmost layer of animal skin, leather that has not been altered, meaning imperfections and idiosyncrasies are fully visible

TOP-GRAIN LEATHER

Hide that has been sanded over or smoothed out, removing visible flaws

PEBBLE-GRAIN OR PEBBLED LEATHER

Leather that has been given a man-made texture of small, round, raised protrusions

PATENT LEATHER

Buffed, smooth, shiny, and reflective leather treated with a high-gloss plastic coating

EMBOSSED LEATHER

Any leather given a man-made pattern, typically applied using heat

SUEDE

Leather from the underside of animal skin that's been given an applied finish described as "napped," meaning it's almost fuzzy or generally not entirely smooth

NUBUCK

Treated to resemble the texture of suede, but from the exterior side of the animal skin, like most other types of leather

Sustainable Alternatives

The world of footwear is nothing if not diverse in its product offerings, and as more of us look for options beyond the traditional styles that have anchored the industry for so long, that diversity extends to the materials used to make shoes. It's now relatively easy to find shoes made from fabrics and materials other than traditional leathers—especially online. Dr. Martens has an entire range of their signature boots and brogues made from synthetic leather, and companies such as Novacas and the London-based Will's Vegan Shoes both use microfibers in their designs, which can easily pass for leather shoes in appearance.

There are even more options if your quest for traditional leather alternatives takes you to casual, everyday sneakers. The French brand Veja makes tennis shoes that incorporate tilapia, with rubber soles sustainably harvested in Brazil using a method that doesn't invoke lasting damage to trees. Adidas makes versions of some of their most popular styles from recycled debris found in the ocean and has also been experimenting with 3-D printed iterations, while Spain's Ecoalf upcycles plastic bottles into sneakers and used tires into flip-flops.

OPEN

CLOSED

OPEN VS. CLOSED

Closed-laced and open-laced shoes are separated by a simple feature that makes a big difference: whether or not the facing is sewn below the vamp (see page 13). The name is derived from the space that open-laced shoes have, an opening created by the small lip. Because closed-laced shoes don't have that opening, their silhouette is a bit sleeker and more streamlined, and, thus, considered more formal than open-laced shoes. See page 64 for lacing ideas.

WEAR A HEEL

Wearing a shoe with a substantial heel is a bold style move. But, even if the heel on your shoe of choice offers minimal lift, it's important to pay attention to how a heel is constructed. Depending on your gait, the heel will likely absorb more shock when walking than any other part of the shoe, placing a premium on durable, sturdy construction.

The most common types of heels in men's dress shoes are made from leather, either stacked or crafted from what's known as fiberboard (essentially, compressed leather scraps molded into a heel shape). Stacked heels are built from multiple thin layers of leather placed atop one another. This method emphasizes precise craftsmanship, which is why you will find stacked heels in footwear made by shoe companies who prize traditional techniques.

In theory, a cobbler can repair stacked heels less invasively, by peeling off damaged layers and replacing them as needed. You can't do that with a fiberboard heel, which has to be replaced in full if it cracks or wears down.

Some shoemakers also use wooden or faux-wooden heels. In addition to usually making the shoe heavier, wooden heels run into the same problem as fiberboard—the only way to repair them is to replace them altogether.

To increase the life of your heel, apply protective taps or pads made from rubber or noisier options made from steel, which will announce your arrival as you enter a room.

Chapter Two

THE
SHOES

HOW TO SHINE A SHOE

Each of the foundational styles of footwear featured in this chapter can be distinguished from the others by observing which parts of the shoe are integral, which are missing, and how they relate to one another. Sometimes the differences are subtle; sometimes they're quite pronounced. And sometimes, innovative designers kick tradition right out the window, creating hybrid shoes that defy classification and, in some cases, logic and the boundaries of good taste. For now, take a look at the most essential types of footwear for an idea of what sets each apart from the rest and which you may still need to add to your wardrobe.

BUSINESS OR BLACK TIE

CLOSED-LACED

LOW HEEL

THE OXFORD

It makes sense to start with one of the most essential, foundational shoes: the oxford. Oxford shoes are what you would most likely envision if you were asked to imagine a simple, sleek dress shoe. Named for the young intellectuals at the University of Oxford, who preferred them to boots, they're straightforward and formal, a can't-fail option to pair with a tuxedo or a suit.

They're always lace-ups—and, as you are now able to recognize by sight after reading chapter 1, they're closed-laced in construction, a key trait that helps differentiate them from other, similar styles. They also always fit under your ankles and, unlike, say, a boot, typically feature a low heel. A Goodyear welt is pretty standard for an oxford shoe, too. But despite all that, there are some ways to add a personal touch that reflects your own sense of style. You can opt for a cap-toe, for example, or you can punch up the type of leather used. Patent leather is the most formal and should probably be reserved for black-tie situations; a matte leather is more versatile if you need to choose just one pair.

TIP If you really want to up your style game, some shoemakers make what are called "whole-cut oxfords," with an upper crafted from one single (and often expensive) piece of leather.

Every time we put on our shoes, we make a statement.

—SÉBASTIEN KOPP,
COFOUNDER OF VEJA

Why Italian Leather Is Considered the Best

If you were to survey 100 people on the street, *Family Feud*–style, to find out where the best leather in the world comes from, you may very well find the majority would say the planet's finest leather is Italian. By and large, this is due to tradition. Italy has a rich heritage of craftspeople who have worked with leather for centuries to create covetable (and expensive) shoes, bags, furniture, and the like. The country is home to some of the most famous luxury houses known for their leather goods—shoes, in particular—such as Tod's, Gucci, and Bruno Magli. Florence has been in many ways the epicenter of the Italian leather trade since at least the thirteenth century; the famed Scuola del Cuoio ("Leather School") has been in operation since just after World War II and still attracts tourists willing to drop a few hundred euros. The city's streets are lined with shops and stalls peddling small leather goods.

In reality, though, quality leather can be found around the world. In the United States, the Horween Leather Company in Chicago has built a highly regarded reputation among shoemakers as a top-notch tannery since it was founded in 1905. The Kyoto Leather Project in Japan aims to marry native Japanese leather with the country's traditional craftsmanship. Independent labels such as New York's Brother Vellies and Canada's Oliberté are also making strides to showcase the type of high-quality leather shoes that can be sourced from African countries, such as Ethiopia, Kenya, and South Africa.

WORK OR EVERYDAY

OPEN-LACED

LOW HEEL

THE DERBY

The derby shoe looks a lot like an oxford, except for one primary difference: The lacing system is open, as opposed to closed. "Historically, derbies have been stiff-leathered, open-laced [shoes] that would be worn with trousers and a sport jacket," explains Byron Peart, who, along with his twin brother, Dexter, founded the leather goods label Want Les Essentiels in 2006; they make a mean selection of derbies themselves. "It's the everyday, comfortable, and versatile shoe that can be worn with anything," adds Dexter. That's true. Derbies are less formal and a bit more rugged than oxfords, which also means that even traditional shoemakers are likely to offer more varieties of derbies in terms of color and materials used. One scroll through a well-stocked e-commerce site, from Mr Porter to Zappos, and you'll find derby shoes in black, brown, navy, beige, and all varieties of suedes and leathers, along with soles of varying thickness. "It's an easy-to-wear option for travel or for the office," Byron says. "It can be dressed up or down according to occasions."

TIP The derby is an ideal choice for reflecting your personal style, although, as always, the simpler the style, the more often you'll find you can wear it.

CAN BE AN OXFORD, DERBY, OR BOOT

DECORATIVE PERFORATIONS | BUSINESS OR EVERYDAY

THE BROGUE

A brogue is not actually a category of shoe in the way that a derby or an oxford is, primarily because a brogue can actually be a derby or an oxford—but not all derbies or oxfords are brogues. Allow us to explain. Broguing is the term used to describe the decorative perforations (the "perfing") or saw-toothed edging ("pinking") sometimes found on a shoe's upper. You have probably come across a pair of wing-tip shoes before—named for the curved, winglike piece of leather that stretches across the upper from the toe to the vamp. Wing-tips are a classic example of a brogue and can be fairly ornate, but even a simple cap-toe shoe with some perforations across the front would qualify for this category. So brogues are any oxford or derby with this type of decorative element.

Keeping in mind the general rule that the more complicated something is, the more casual it becomes, brogues that are oxfords are a step down on the formality meter from their unadorned oxford brothers. That doesn't make them a bad starter option, though. "Chocolate-brown brogues will work with most styles and colors of suit—just not black suits or eveningwear," says Dan Rookwood of Mr Porter, "as well as with smart indigo denim or dark-colored chinos, cords, or moleskins." Sounds like a pretty good argument for getting a pair.

BUCKLE CLOSURE | BUSINESS OR EVERYDAY

THE MONK STRAP

This one is pretty easy to spot in the wild. In short, monk strap shoes are fastened with buckles rather than laces. Most commonly, this means one to two straps with closures on the outward-facing side of the shoe, although some designers will add three, four, or even more. If you're feeling so bold as to purchase a triple monk strap shoe, far be it from us to cramp your style. But, practically speaking, single or double monk straps are a much savvier buy, from a timelessness standpoint; they won't look like a passing fad or like they're trying too hard. The look is distinctive enough, so choose options that are fairly streamlined, otherwise in neutral colors, with a cap-toe if you'd like to throw in a little flair. Alternatively, you can wear them like the well-dressed Italians who helped make this shoe popular in recent years and leave the top strap undone for a carefree air of nonchalance.

TIP Even from one single monk strap shoe to another, buckle placement can vary. For the most classic look, opt for those with buckles that sit just to the side of where laces would be.

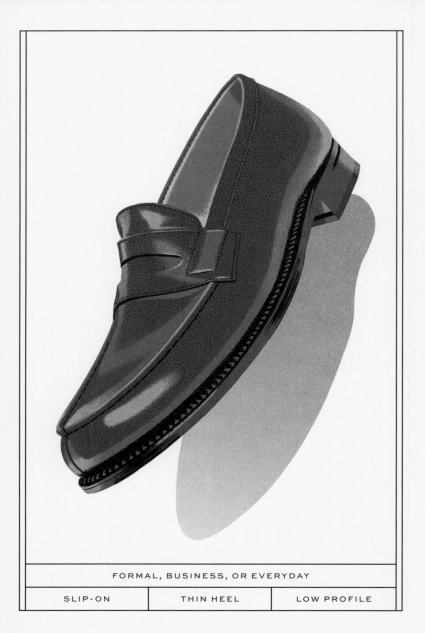

FORMAL, BUSINESS, OR EVERYDAY

| SLIP-ON | THIN HEEL | LOW PROFILE |

THE LOAFER

Loafers can come adorned with many different decorations—tassels, a slot for a penny, a metal bar or chain across the saddle—but the basics are unchanged. Loafers are laceless, low in profile, and usually have a thin heel. That makes them easy to slip on and equally easy to wear. "Every guy needs the perfect cordovan loafer," says Eric Jennings, vice president and fashion director at Saks Fifth Avenue. (Cordovan is a type of nonporous horse leather.) "It can be worn dressed up with a suit, or worn casual with jeans. The cordovan color is the perfect shade, between black and brown, so it goes well with everything." Be careful, though: Because loafers generally sit on a thin sole, pay extra attention to construction and leather quality if you plan to wear them out on the town.

TIP Some guys will wear their loafers as slip-ons, folding the back heel down inside and sliding their foot in over it. If that's a look you like, you can buy loafers with collapsible heels made especially for that reason.

The penny loafer is the ultimate shoe. They are comfortable and versatile: You can wear them with a suit to a meeting; you can wear them with old Levi's to get a coffee. Always have pennies situated in the slot where they belong. It brings good luck. Bonus points if the pennies are from the year you were born.

—CHRIS BLACK, WRITER AND LOAFER ENTHUSIAST

The Classic Gucci Loafer

In the pantheon of these formal slip-ons, one very clearly stands out above the rest: the Gucci loafer. Like so many other high-end designer labels, Gucci has seen its popularity ebb and flow since it was founded in Florence, Italy, in 1921, and over the years it has admittedly introduced some truly questionable items (see: a men's sparkly green bodysuit open below the belly button).

But throughout it all, their signature leather loafer remains a reliable cornerstone, with a standard offering in buttery-soft black or brown leather that changes only ever so slightly season after season. Handcrafted in Italy, the loafers are easy to spot, thanks to a simple metal clasp across the front, known as the horsebit. The story goes that the brand's founder, the amazingly named Guccio Gucci, included motifs that referenced the equestrian world in his product to appeal to English aristocrats. The plan worked and then some; the signature Gucci loafer was introduced in 1953 and has been seen on everyone with money to spend, from Leonardo DiCaprio in *The Wolf of Wall Street* to A$AP Rocky outside of a fashion show. So, yes, if you purchase a Gucci loafer, you are paying for a bit of that borrowed prestige and a history of swanky, jet-set appeal. But you're also paying for shoes made with incredible attention to detail and built—still by hand!—to last.

EVERYDAY

FEW EYELETS, IF ANY

HIGHER HEEL

THE DRESS BOOT

The category of dress boot can be broken down to include several styles, but most relevant if you're planning to dress up is the Chelsea boot. Identified by its height—it hits above the ankle—and by its construction—most have a higher heel and either a zipper on the innermost side or a band of elastic on both sides—the Chelsea boot can add a little rock-'n'-roll finesse to your suit or when worn with jeans. A lot less formal (and a bit less versatile) is the chukka or desert boot. While chukka boots do have laces, they have only a few eyelets. The material used and type of sole you choose go a long way in determining how dressy chukkas can be: A suede boot with a crepe sole (a textured sole made from rubber) is at the casual end of the spectrum, opposite from a style that uses a leather sole and a polished leather upper.

TIP Before you take your boots out on the town, make sure you have socks in your wardrobe that are taller. They will help you avoid chafing on your calves as you're breaking them in (and steer clear of flashing an awkward swath of bare leg when you sit down).

EVERYDAY

THICK SOLE | HIGH PROFILE

THE WORK BOOT

A work boot is any boot that is designed for you to actually do physical work—or at least look like you might—while wearing them. Think Timberlands, CAT Footwear, Wolverine boots, or Red Wings. Some people may even include cowboy boots here, although we are likely to put them in their own special, country-western-flavored category. It's a broad grouping, either way, and if you wear work boots off of the construction site or trail (or rodeo, as the case may be), know they have no place in any kind of formal setting or with a suit, unless you need to maybe give a press conference outside during a snowstorm. Otherwise, keep your recreational work boot wear casual.

TIP Even though work boots are made to take a beating, they can benefit from some extra love like any other footwear you own. Applying waterproofing spray or wax designed specifically for the type of boots you have can give them some extra life.

EVERYDAY | RUBBER SOLE

When I gave up drugs I had to obsess about something, and I'm not into cars, not into jewelry, and I had loads of guitars, so I set off on a quest to collect Adidas trainers.

—NOEL GALLAGHER, TO *THE INDEPENDENT*

THE SNEAKER

Yes, the sneaker. Or the trainer, as the Brits say. Rubber-soled, known for comfort or for performance, sneakers are ideal for everyday wear. And, lucky for us all, it has become more and more acceptable to wear sneakers in places where they were once forbidden. Traditionalists may see this as the slow breakdown of society, but the truth remains: Sneakers are just as important a part of any man's wardrobe as are more formal shoes. (And there are times when you can wear a pair of sneakers with a suit—we'll get to that later.) The most timeless, most versatile sneakers to make sure you have in your closet are a plain white pair with minimal branding and even fewer distracting design elements. But even with those parameters, your choices are vast.

TIP Some of the most timeless sneakers—Chuck Taylors, Stan Smiths, the Nike Cortez—are also relatively inexpensive. If you can swing it, buy two at once: one for everyday wear and one to keep fresh for when scuffs just won't do.

The Eternal Appeal of White Tennies

Let's get one truth out of the way: A plain white tennis shoe can be worn with nearly everything the average man will wear in his lifetime. This is a bold statement, but think about it in practical terms. White, the most neutral of colors, coordinates seamlessly with other colors. If the sneakers you choose are one of the classics—like, say, a pair of Adidas Stan Smiths or a more recent addition to the Sneaker Hall of Fame, such as the Common Projects Achilles— you won't be hampered by flashy branding or other come-and-go, trendy design flourishes, giving your footwear a certain timeless appeal.

Their very plainness is what makes them so endlessly appropriate; there's nothing tying these shoes to a specific occasion or moment, making them extremely versatile. And since they're sneakers and should, by definition, offer some cushion and support, you should want to wear them everywhere you can.

So, yes, you can wear them with jeans. You can wear them with other trousers. You can wear them with or without socks. You can wear them with a suit, if decorum and dress codes allow. You probably can't wear them with a tux, really, but go ahead and try, if that's your thing. Just make sure you're ready to go home and change if you get turned away at the door. But the good news is that you'll be in sneakers; you can jog home and be back in no time.

Chapter Three

STEPPING UP YOUR STYLE

HOW TO SHINE A SHOE

Geographically speaking, your pants sit right above your shoes, and, therefore, how well the two coordinate will be key to whether you look like a million bucks or like a soggy dollar bill. Unless you're in the market for an entirely new wardrobe, it's not a bad idea to take stock of the pants you already own before pulling the trigger on a new set of shoes. Here are some helpful guidelines for fail-safe combinations for your lower half, along with some rules of thumb for things to avoid.

JEANS

•

To crib from those old TV ads for cotton, denim is the fabric of many of our daily lives. That's convenient, because they can be worn with a wide variety of footwear.

YES TO
derbies, chukka boots, Chelsea boots, work boots, sneakers

NO TO
oxfords

PROCEED WITH CAUTION
loafers

PRO-TIPS
- The color of your jeans matters. Darker denim reads dressier; it's generally a safer bet to pair light jeans with sneakers.

- Similarly, the color of your shoes is important, too. Browns will usually work better than blacks.

- The more distressing you have going on with your jeans, the more you should err on the side of sneakers.

- Suede and denim pair nicely; polished or patent leathers may send you into the danger zone.

- If you'd like to wear your loafers with denim, opt for jeans on the skinny side.

- Take note from Mr Porter's Dan Rookwood: "I would never wear oxfords with jeans. There is too big a disconnect in formality there."

TROUSERS

Trousers is an admittedly huge category that includes everything from pants in corduroy or wool to khakis and more. So there is some flexibility here, depending on exactly which type of trousers you're considering. For simplicity's sake, though, we'll break down some easy guidelines.

YES TO
oxfords, derbies, loafers, monk straps, Chelsea boots, sneakers

PROCEED WITH CAUTION
work boots

PRO-TIPS

- Wearing a pair of trousers is a great place to let your derbies shine; it's what they're made for.

- Less formal oxfords (e.g., not patent leather) can also work, although there is a larger margin of error to getting it just right.

- Keep in mind that, as with denim, the looser the trouser is at the ankle, the less likely a thin-soled, narrow shoe will look good.

- Colorwise, a good point of reference is to ensure that your trousers complement the hue of your shoes but don't match perfectly; a little contrast goes a long way.

- Rugged work boots are best paired with denim or the type of heavy-duty, utilitarian trousers made by brands such as Dickies or Carhartt.

A SUIT

Suits, like dress shoes, come in all colors, patterns, and silhouettes. But even with the variety available, there are some hard-and-fast rules that are worth following.

YES TO
oxfords, derbies, loafers

NO TO
work boots

PROCEED WITH CAUTION
chukka boots, Chelsea boots, sneakers

PRO-TIPS

- Oxfords and suits go together like peas and carrots. Don't question it too much; it's worked for generations and will work well for you, too.

- Here's a time when a little shine on your shoes can be your friend (see page 88).

- If you do opt for sneakers (see page 55), keep them simple, clean, and unadorned. Minimalism is key.

- Loafers and derbies are more casual, so if the occasion isn't quite so stuffy, feel free to give yours a whirl.

- Black suits pair well with black shoes; gray, navy, and brown suits paired with brown shoes will give you a polished look, too.

I really think guys only need two pairs of shoes. A nice pair of black shoes and a pair of Chuck Taylors.

—MINDY KALING, *IS EVERYONE HANGING OUT WITHOUT ME?*

Well-Suited Sneakers

In case you're wondering, you can wear sneakers with a suit. As we've generally moved toward a more casual mode of dress as a society and workplace dress codes have relaxed, the idea of wearing sneakers with a suit, which may have seemed like an outlandish cry for attention generations ago, is fairly acceptable in many circumstances these days.

As mentioned, minimalist, pristine white sneakers are the gold standard here. They'll work regardless of the color of your suit or the fabric from which it has been made. You'll have to read the room a little to determine how tying on your trainers will be received, but keep in mind that owning a suit that is well tailored and fits you perfectly is a must in order to truly pull off the formal sneakers look. Otherwise, it's easy to step into "he's just sloppy" territory.

A TUX

You can't easily replicate the feeling of getting dressed to the nines in a tuxedo to celebrate something that warrants putting on your finest. And so you'll want to make sure you look flawless, from bow tie to toe.

YES TO
oxfords

NO TO
almost everything else

PROCEED WITH CAUTION
velvet slippers

PRO-TIPS

- While rules are made to be broken, here's one you can rely on: The most formal outfit you can wear is a tuxedo; unless you're a sartorial revolutionary hell-bent on making a bold fashion statement, opt for coordinating yours with oxfords, the most formal of footwear.

- You will see men with a confident sense of style pairing their tuxes with a luxe set of velvet slippers. It's a look that's bold and louche; if those are adjectives you use to describe yourself, you might consider a pair. But if you're interested in investing in shoes you'll have plenty of opportunity to wear, skip those for now.

SHORTS

If it's hot enough to wear shorts, it's hot enough to consider footwear that's breathable in warm weather. Hint: That means suede usually doesn't apply.

YES TO
sneakers, boat shoes

NO TO
almost everything else

PROCEED WITH CAUTION
flip-flops and sandals

PRO-TIPS

- An unequivocal truism is that sneakers, specifically low-top sneakers, worn with shorts will look better than any other kind of footwear worn with shorts. Any place you can wear shorts, sneakers will suffice.

- Boat shoes (leather or canvas low-tops with a rubber sole initially designed to be worn on deck) are a preppy symbol of all things summer that you can also sub in here. Be warned, though: They're meant to be worn without socks, which means if you wear them in the heat often, you'll need to invest in some no-show socks (Sperry makes a good pair with silicone to prevent them from slipping) or else air them out regularly.

- Sandals and flip-flops are often derided by traditionalists as not suitable to wear in any setting that isn't a poolside or at the beach. You can determine how you feel about that rule; but do consider that wearing them around town will likely ensure that your feet will end up filthy at the end of the day.

USE A SHOEHORN

A shoehorn is a simple tool that men often overlook when getting dressed each morning that can not only make fitting into a pair of snug shoes a bit easier, but also help you maintain the shape of your leather shoes and, in turn, keep them looking fresh longer.

For the uninitiated, a shoehorn is a flat, smooth tool with rounded edges that you insert between the heel of your foot and the inside heel of your shoe to help your foot slide in with little resistance. You can find shoehorns crafted from a variety of materials, from plastic and metal to those made from animal horn or hooves to glass (which seems precarious) and even stone. Some come adorned with long handles, landing the act of putting on your shoes at the top of your list of least strenuous activities.

But, as mentioned above, there are some other benefits. Leather, especially before it's been broken in, can be stiff and not terribly pliable. Shoving your foot into a stiff leather shoe without a shoehorn can bend, buckle, or crush the heel portion of the upper, causing it to lose shape sooner than it would naturally, even if the leather is soft. A shoehorn alleviates that problem and also prevents you from having to unlace your shoes through the top few eyelets before putting them on or having to bend down and crease your freshly pressed trousers. It's a tiny hack that can make an outsized difference.

1

If your shoes have laces, loosen the top eyelets, leaving the laces untied.

2

Holding the shoehorn by its handle, insert it inside the back of the shoe, where the back of your ankle will meet the interior heel portion of the upper.

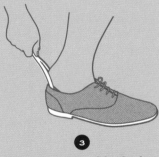

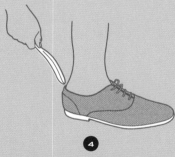

3

Without letting go of the shoehorn, slide your foot over it and into the shoe, as though it's going down a playground slide. If needed, you can use the shoehorn to gently stretch the heel back to allow more room for your foot to get inside, but be careful not to fold the heel portion of the upper.

4

Once your foot is in, gently remove the shoehorn, tie your laces, and get on with your life!

KEEP IT COMFY

It's to be expected that the more time you spend on your feet, the more likely you are to experience some sort of discomfort in your footwear. Even the softest, most supportive sneaker can cause pain if you're standing or walking all day long. But there is one very easy, cost-effective solution to small foot woes: insoles.

Think of insoles like a Band-Aid for your feet. If you have minor discomfort, an insole—a soft, thin, cushioned layer you buy separately and insert inside your shoe under the foot—can offer some relief. Insoles absorb shock, decreasing the stress you feel from heel to toe. They're often inexpensive; Dr. Scholl's, a well-known insole manufacturer for over a century, offers versions for $10.

Before you purchase, make sure there's enough room in your shoe for an added layer of cushioning. If not, you may need to size up, or at least break in your shoes a bit more. Test them out for short periods of time first, so you can adjust to how they feel.

If the problem causing your foot pain is chronic, you may need to consider a different type of shoe with more arch support. Foot stress can lead to pain elsewhere in your body (often your back), so it's not a bad idea to consult a doctor if the problem is consistent.

Socks or No Socks?

Going sockless isn't a suitable option for every shoe. It works best with below-the-ankle shoes, such as loafers or oxfords and derbies, and is a decidedly casual stance to take (i.e., don't do it at a black-tie wedding, but a less formal wedding, like one held outdoors during the day, for example, could be a good place). The look also tends to pair better with pants that are cuffed and hemmed closer around your ankles, where the effect will appear intentional.

"The following styles of footwear should be worn without socks," says Dan Rookwood of Mr Porter. "Leather sandals, dress slippers, espadrilles, boat shoes, and (when poolside or on the beach) flip-flops." He continues, "You can expose your ankles for a cool summery look when wearing other shoes such as tennis shoes, slip-on sneakers, loafers, or even hard-soled shoes, such as brogues and monk straps."

Saks Fifth Avenue's Eric Jennings adheres to a stricter set of guidelines. "Going sockless will hurt your feet and destroy the smell of your shoes," he warns. "I only go sockless if I'm wearing sandals." Eric offers a popular middle ground: the no-show sock, which covers your toes and heels but isn't high enough to peek out from over the tops of your shoes. "Don't bother with the colorful, striped versions," he says. "No one will see them, so just go with white or black."

If you do go au naturel, consider buying an odor-eating spray to apply to the inside of the shoe at the end of the day. And if you have super-pale skin, consider a tan, too. Providing a blinding flash of ultra-white ankle is probably not the effect you're going for.

HOW TO
LACE 'EM UP

There are probably an infinite amount of ways to lace up your shoes, but there are three styles you'll most likely need on a regular basis. As mentioned in chapter 1, thin laces are generally preferable to thick ones for dress shoes, as they give a cleaner, more polished look, and rounded laces are considered more formal than their flat counterparts. If you need a refresher, flip back to page 13, and take a look at the definitions for eyelets and facing. You may also want to review the difference between closed- and open-laced construction from the same section.

BAR LACING

This style of lacing is named for the straight parallel lines the laces form across the top of the shoe, from left to right. This is the traditional, formal method for lacing oxfords (which are closed-laced shoes, if you recall).

1

2

Evenly thread the lace into the bottom two eyelets, so that the lace ends sit beneath the facing but above the tongue.

Thread the right lace end up through the next available eyelet, across the facing, and into the eyelet directly opposite. Repeat on the left.

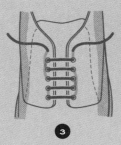

3

Continue this lacing technique until you reach the top pair of eyelets. If your shoes have an odd number of eyelets, you'll need to cross them diagonally underneath the facing so they end up on opposite sides of the shoe, enabling you to tie them in a simple bow.

CRISSCROSS LACING

For derbies, you can also try crisscross lacing. This technique is a bit more youthful and comfortable—after all, it is the style you see most often in sneakers.

1

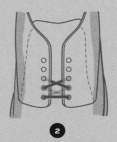

2

Start with the first step of bar lacing: Thread an evenly distributed amount of lace into the bottom eyelets, underneath the facing and over the tongue.

Then alternate lacing through the eyelets on each side, but—and this is important—always up from underneath the facing. So that means the right side passes across the tongue, goes up through the first eyelet on the left from underneath, and the left side travels up through the first eyelet on the right. They then cross at the tongue, passing underneath the facing on the opposite side and up through the next set of eyelets.

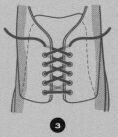

3

Continue until you reach the top eyelets and have enough left over to tie in a bow.

OVER-UNDER LACING

This is the easiest, fastest, and probably the most intuitive way to lace your shoes . . . which also means it's the most casual. Try it out for sneakers. This method is very similar to crisscross lacing, except you can ignore the concept of always lacing from the bottom of the facing up through the eyelets. Instead, you can alternate coming up from the bottom of the facing and in from the top.

1

Start the same way as bar lacing—thread an evenly distributed amount of lace downward into the bottom eyelet, underneath the facing and over the tongue.

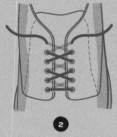

2

Then simply feed each side of the lace over the tongue up through opposite eyelets, across the top of the facing and back down into the eyelet on the other side. It will still look neat, but the effect denotes convenience more than style.

BEND THE RULES

Feeling a little stifled by all the rules we've proposed you follow in this book? If that's the case, then this section is for you. Here we've lined up a three-part process. One: We've provided some common and oft-repeated style laws that many experts claim you should follow religiously. Two: We offer our two cents on whether you should listen to them. And three: We leave you to make up your own mind.

TUCK YOUR PANTS INTO YOUR BOOTS

Soldiers do it. Cowboys do it. So should you? That's going to be a no from us, sir. We hesitate to ever say "never," but this one is probably as close as we will get to advising you to wholeheartedly and steadfastly avoid a styling trick. Not only does it seem uncomfortable, but it telegraphs someone who is trying very hard to make a bold style statement. And nothing is less cool than looking like you're trying too hard.

MATCH YOUR BELT TO YOUR SHOES

This one is pretty basic: Many men are taught, at some point in their lives, that their belt should always coordinate precisely with their footwear. And while that's never a bad choice, it doesn't need to be executed with such life-or-death accuracy. "The leather should 'agree,'" says Dan Rookwood of Mr Porter, meaning different shades of brown together, for example, are acceptable. "It doesn't necessarily have to directly match. The only thing I would say is never wear brown and black leather together."

Beyond a belt, don't think too hard about matching your shoes to other accessories, either. It's more important that your tie coordinates with your shirt than your brogues, for example, and that your cuff links don't clash with your watch. The great thing about black or brown leather shoes is that they're neutral, after all.

AVOID WHITE SHOES

We aren't talking about white sneakers here, which we've already noted are actually preferable to sneakers in other colors. We're talking white dress shoes. While black and brown are often given credence as the only two truly worthy options, and navy, beige, or even oxblood can be tolerated, white is cited by some experts as a strict no-go. "I love white shoes—proper shoes, like bucks," says David Coggins, an author and men's style connoisseur. "They have a sense of occasion—it feels like you're celebrating the season when you wear them. I have some pairs I've never even worn yet. They're sitting in my closet like a prince waiting for the day when he can take the throne." If that's not a royal endorsement, we don't know what is.

STRAY FROM BLACK SOCKS

We've already mentioned that you can go sockless if you like (or choose a no-show sock). But if you do throw on some men's hosiery—again, except when wearing sneakers—common sense dictates you should go black or at least a dark navy. You wouldn't be completely wrong; those choices are hard to discredit. And with a tux, darker is better.

SOCK IT TO THEM

For less formal affairs, socks in plaids, stripes, argyles, and polka dots (especially small ones) are just as traditional as solid colors. You can begin by experimenting a bit with those patterns in blues and blacks, if you'd like, before moving on to eye-catching designs or colors.

Traditionalists in black or navy socks may not ever need to consider coordinating them with their ties, since those colors match pretty much everything. Whether you want to get into that level of detail is a matter of personal taste, but it will help you appear more pulled together if you do, especially if you're going to be sitting down and your socks will be exposed. If you do match your socks to your neckwear, keep the

relationship casual. Think complementary colors (ones opposite each other on the color wheel), as opposed to precisely matching patterns or prints. The extra effort will show you care, but exact matches can leave you looking a bit like a circus clown. (No disrespect to Bozo.)

Beyond that, and especially if you move in spaces where people aren't so rigid about style rules, we say go crazy. Life's too short to worry about whether patterned socks are going to be okay.

BREAK IN YOUR SHOES

If you ask, you'll be offered many different solutions for breaking in your shoes. But the simplest answer is usually the best: You just need to wear them. Depending on how stiff the leather is, you may want to start small, with a trip back and forth to the store or a morning commute. This method will help the shoe break in in relation to the precise way your foot moves. Be prepared with Band-Aids, strategically cut moleskin, or thick socks to fight blisters or chafing—and an alternate pair of shoes to change into to give your feet a break.

If that fails, you can get creative. Shoe stretchers—wooden inserts that you can crank to loosen tight leather, like a medieval torture device—are inexpensive and easy to find online. You can also stuff your shoes with damp—*not soaked*—newspaper to soften them before wearing. Many online sites offer the "life hack" of applying a blow dryer to the shoes while you're wearing them, which makes the leather more pliable. Be cautious, though: Prolonged, direct, dry heat is never a good match for leather or suede.

HEM YOUR PANTS

The "break," in tailoring parlance, means the point at which the hem of your pants meets your shoes. Over the last few decades, various trends—and coordinating trendsetters—have dictated everything from "full break" pants, which hit the shoe with enough excess length to cause a fold in the bottom of the pants, to cropped pants, which stop well above the ankle.

Flip the page for a breakdown—pun intended—to help you decide which style works for you. Breaks come in degrees, since tailors can give you just as much of one, or as little, as you like, but they generally fall into three categories: full, half, or no break at all. Just remember: The more excessive the break, the more confidence and attention to pant fit is required. You'll want to prove that this was an intentional choice and not the result of a reckless tailor.

FULL BREAK

When the hem is long enough that it easily touches the tops of your shoes, it causes a slight concave fold around the ankle. Despite this old-school cut being generous in length, the hem of your pants should still never spill over the shoe heel and hit the ground.

HALF-BREAK

Here, the hem hits the top of your shoes, but only just enough that there is a slight concave fold, visible from the front. When in doubt, a small break like this is widely accepted; it will keep you looking neat and sleek, particularly in a suit.

NO BREAK

Trousers with no break never make contact with your shoes, exposing your sock or ankle. This is a bolder look that works better when pants are tapered. The higher the crop, the riskier the pants are to wear.

> **TIP** *When discussing the break of your pants, your tailor may also ask about a cuff. There's no compelling reason why you should have one, especially if your pants are tailored to your height specifically. However, if you do opt for cuffs, keep them simple and narrow. Bigger isn't always better, and you can get a streamlined look much more easily without cuffed pants.*

Play it safe: A small break is best as it helps hide the skin above a man's sock while at the same time conforms to today's trend.

—ALAN DAVID,
FOURTH-GENERATION TAILOR

Chapter Four

CARING FOR
YOUR SHOES

HOW TO SHINE A SHOE

Shoes require maintenance; there's really no two ways about it. But don't let that be a deterrent to investing in a pair you like. When all is said and done, shoe care is less of a time commitment than maintaining a houseplant, and is likely to garner you more compliments than keeping a succulent alive would, too.

With that in mind, here are some insider tips and tricks of the trade you can use for your oxfords, derbies, and whatever other footwear you acquire.

THINK OUTSIDE THE BOX

Sneaker collectors, notoriously one of the most obsessive of all the footwear aficionados, will often go to extremes to keep their Jordans and limited-edition kicks du jour in "box fresh" condition. This can include measures as meticulous as airtight boxes, display cases, and steam-sealed plastic wrap. Those efforts are effective but not terribly practical. You can take their modes of storage down a few notches and still take great care to keep your shoes in good condition for as long as possible.

Shoe trees are functional and low-maintenance, and can be inexpensive. You can think of a shoe tree as a wooden foot, in essence, that serves to help maintain the shape of your shoes when you aren't wearing them. You simply slide one into each shoe after you take them off and keep them in there until you wear them again. The best options are made from wood that also absorbs moisture to keep leather fresh. Cedar is considered optimal for its superior wicking ability, and it smells pretty nice, too.

Higher-end shoes will often come with a shoe bag. If you store your shoes in them, you'll keep dust off, but they're mostly convenient for travel, to avoid nicks and scuffs from whatever else might be next to them in your luggage.

Depending on what the storage space in your home allows, it's not a bad idea to keep shoes in the boxes they come in when you purchase them. It helps you stay organized and helps you avoid damaging them in your closet. If you do use a shoebox or a shoe bag, make sure your shoes are dry when you put them away. Dampness in the confines of a dark, warm shoe box is a breeding ground for bacteria. You can purchase stackable plastic shoeboxes with drop-front openings that you can leave undone to help air out your shoes—but even that isn't a replacement for simply waiting until they're completely dry before you put them away.

If you purchase taller boots, consider stuffing them with paper before putting them away. Depending on the stiffness and height of the boot in question, they may tip to one side when left without reinforcement, which can create creases and wrinkles that weaken the leather (and look pretty bad, too).

CLEAN YOUR SHOES

Shoes take a beating sometimes, even when it's unplanned. Depending on how you spend your time, the everyday perils threatening the cleanliness of your shoes might include assailants such as rain, rock salt, mud, or red wine spills. Here are some best practices to get rid of all types of excess grime.

IT'S ALL FUN AND GAMES 'TIL IT RAINS

All is not lost if you do find yourself caught in a thunderstorm. Once you're inside, take your shoes off and insert a shoe tree to make sure they retain their shape while they dry. You can also stuff them with newspaper, which will help wick away moisture. There are readily available leather lotions and balms on the market specifically designed to help remove water damage, too, and homemade remedies, such as a mix of equal parts water and vinegar, can sometimes help lift water marks. Whatever you do, don't use a hair dryer or put your shoes directly into a dryer—that will likely do more harm than good.

If you believe in taking precautionary measures, there are companies that make rubber overshoes or galoshes that you can slip over your loafers or lace-ups and then remove once you arrive at your destination. (Swims is a popular overshoe choice.) Suede and nubuck are particularly susceptible to rain damage, so it's not a bad idea to treat them in advance by applying a waterproofing spray that you can usually find in shoe stores and online for about $10.

INVEST IN A SUEDE BRUSH (OR TWO)

Suede can be less forgiving than other materials when it comes to removing stains, so it helps to have a few brushes in your arsenal. A soft-bristled brush can be used to lightly scrub away loose dirt or dried mud; when applied gently, it won't damage the suede. If it leaves the suede looking flat afterward, wait until it's dry and then use a brush made from stiffer materials. "I recommend a suede shoe brush with brass bristles," says Eric Jennings of Saks Fifth Avenue. "It re-fluffs the suede pile and brings the shoes back to their best after they've been worn a while."

IT'S OK TO USE DISH SOAP ON LEATHER

Moderation is key—a little bit of dish soap will go a long way. If you're nervous, dilute it with water first, and gently dab stains. Never apply too much pressure, and resist the urge to aggressively work a stain back and forth. You can always go in again for a second round once the leather has dried. And don't forget to remove the soap with a bit of warm water afterward—don't let it dry on there, as that will leave a visible mark, too. Then dab it dry with a clean cloth.

FOR TOUGH STAINS, GET CREATIVE

There are plenty of online resources that will advise you to use concoctions of all types to remedy stains on your shoes. Always proceed with caution, testing in small amounts before going in whole hog. Footwear experts will tell you toothpaste can remove stubborn marks, baking soda (also a remedy for odor) can help absorb oil, and a mild shampoo can help with that, too. A mixture of water and vinegar usually works on rock salt (used to prevent sidewalks from icing over in winter) that your shoes may have taken home with them. To clear scuff marks off patent leather, try a dab of olive oil on a damp cloth.

SPECIALITY PRODUCTS EXIST FOR A REASON

Store-bought products specifically tailored for different types of materials are readily available for those who are less inclined to mix up DIY solutions. You can find suede shampoo in shoe stores and online, for example, along with leather cleaners. Separate leather conditioners can be applied after cleaning as a barrier to avoid damage in the future. Jason Markk has an entire range of shoe-cleaning products geared toward satisfying the most discerning customer (read: full-fledged sneaker fanatics).

YOU CAN BLEACH WHITE SNEAKERS

White sneakers attract more than their fair share of visible marks, since they're, you know, white. Dilute bleach in water to make sure it's ultra-mild and use the corner of a rag or a toothbrush to spot-clean stains. And if all else fails, you can put white sneakers in the washing machine. Remove the laces first; use mild detergent on a warm, gentle cycle; and always, always let them air-dry.

SHINE YOUR SHOES

Polishing leather shoes seems like a lost art. Let's not let it die out on our watch, though. Keeping your shoes polished shows you care enough to present shoes that are fresh and shiny, no matter how old they are. And you do care about your new shoes, don't you?

It's worth noting that we aren't talking about suede or patent leather here. By its nature, you can't polish suede, but to restore the shine of your patent-leather shoes, you can simply buff them with a damp cloth.

For other leathers, you have some options. You can purchase a prepackaged shoe-shine kit, which will come with polish, a cloth, and a brush at a minimum. More advanced packages will include several brushes (one for the upper, one for the welt) and different polish options, along with a leather conditioner and possibly other cleaning supplies and tools such as a shoehorn (page 60). If you don't want to shell out the cash for a full kit, you can sub in an old T-shirt for a cloth (warning: It will get stained). You can do a semi-decent job with a toothbrush in dire straits, particularly on the welt of your shoe, but a brush with hard bristles is ideal. Unfortunately, there's really no substitute for shoe polish.

There are plenty of polish options on the market, but a cream or wax polish should do the trick. A wax variety will give you more shine. Keep in mind that you'll need different color polishes for different color shoes.

1

2

Assemble your polish, brush or brushes, and cloth. Fill a glass with water and grab an extra rag for drying. Shoe polish can stain sofas, floors, furniture, and carpets, so if you're doing this indoors, throw down a drop cloth or newspapers.

Make sure your shoes are clean and dry (page 84). Otherwise, you won't be polishing them so much as just rubbing dirt around. Remove any laces, and if you own any shoe trees, insert them to help keep the shape. Otherwise, you can hold the shoe while polishing by putting your nondominant hand inside it.

3

4

Dip a portion of your cloth into the polish and rub it in small circles on the outside of the shoe (minus the sole), until the entirety is covered. Let it sit for a bit; ten minutes should suffice.

Grab your brush and buff your heart out, working the surface of the shoe with a bit of force. A brush with stiff bristles will require less time and effort before you start to notice a healthy shine develop.

⑤

If you want even more shine, you can apply what's called a "spit shine" finish. After buffing off the excess polish, drop a little bit of water directly onto the shoe. Use your cloth to work it in, along with a dab of extra polish.

⑥

When you've achieved the level of polish to satisfy all of your shiniest desires, let the shoes dry before relacing them. There shouldn't be much excess polish left on the shoe, so drying shouldn't take more than twenty minutes. And then you're good to go, like new.

An Argument for Beat-Up Shoes

By the time you finish reading this book, you will have all the knowledge you need to keep your shoes looking crisp and new for as long as you can. But, as with so many other things in life, your shoes can stay fresh and new for only so long—and that might not be a bad thing. Among a certain group of stylish men, beat-up, worn-in, and knocked-around shoes are a sign of a life well lived.

"As much as I like them and for as much as I spend on them, I should treat my shoes better," admits Aaron Levine, senior vice president of design at Abercrombie & Fitch. "I should put shoe trees in them. I should polish them more regularly. The fact is, I buy beautiful shoes made in wonderful factories, and then beat the hell out of them."

The reasoning behind this school of thought isn't that taking care of your belongings is overrated; it's that as shoes age and wear, they become more of an extension of you. "As they get dirty, they begin to reflect your history with them and look even better," says David Coggins.

In other words, not worrying too much about a little dirt and a few stray scuffs could be a way to unlock your own personal style. "Life is short," Aaron says. "Buy things that make you feel good, wear them well, and they will start to take on your own personality."

KNOW WHEN TO RESOLE

Determining when to take your shoes to a cobbler to have them resoled is not that difficult. You will be able to tell by flipping the shoe over if the sole is wearing thin, coming apart, or, at worst, has developed some holes. Even if you don't notice by sight as the wear and tear is occurring, you'll feel problems like these as you walk.

The slightly trickier question is whether it's better to pay to have them repaired or to splurge on a new pair. This may be a matter of cost analysis: How much did you pay for the shoes and how much is your cobbler going to charge you to repair them? And how much will a new pair set you back? It could also involve some sentimentality, especially if the shoes happen to be a pair you really like.

There are some commonsense variables that will determine how soon you may be in the market for resoling: primarily, how often and where you wear your shoes. As noted earlier, rigorous daily use necessitates extra attention in choosing a shoe made with tough construction techniques that can also be resoled, such as Goodyear-welted shoes.

Each time you resole your shoes, think of it as research toward making smart purchases down the line. If the pair you buy starts falling apart in a matter of months, look into other construction methods (and probably a different shoemaker, too). But it's inevitable that shoes will need repairs to their soles at some point. "I firmly believe in buying the best shoes you can afford and keeping them for as long as you can," menswear expert David Coggins says. "I've had shoes resoled many times—it's almost a badge of honor."

FIND A GOOD COBBLER

A good cobbler can prove indispensable. And so it's worth taking time to find one that you trust in your town. Like with any other businesses, you can read reviews of most shoe-repair services online to gauge general customer satisfaction, especially if you're in a pinch and don't have the luxury of comparison-shopping when you need a quick repair. But if you are able to get out and explore your local cobblerverse, asking some key questions first can help you eliminate some guesswork.

ASK AROUND

Talk to friends, family, and coworkers to see if they have a go-to shoe-repair service. Most skilled cobblers should be able to repair shoes of all types, so don't think you need to ask only people with collections of shoes that are similar to yours. Additionally, if you buy your footwear from a brick-and-mortar store, the salespeople may offer a repair service on-site (and it might even be complimentary) or at least know of a reputable cobbler nearby.

UNDERSTAND WHAT A COBBLER CAN DO

The specific skillset of any cobbler can vary. For example, some may be adept at everything from resoling shoes to weatherproofing them, stretching small shoes to fit bigger feet, repairing the buckles on monk straps, or even breaking your footwear in for you. But not all cobblers can do all things. Before presenting your cobbler with your shoe that needs repairing, try to get a sense of what he or she offers.

HAVE AN IDEA OF WHAT YOU NEED

Even if you aren't sure of how to fix your problem, at least go in with a sense of what you think needs to be done. For example, if your heel is a problem area, you may not need the entire sole replaced. If the front of your sole is worn down, a half-heel replacement may be sufficient—and will save you money. If a cobbler offers more, ask him to explain why and judge that explanation accordingly.

BE MINDFUL OF TURNAROUND TIME

Shoe repair is an artisanal business that may take time. Use some common sense: If your repairs sound extensive, question if a short turnaround seems like it might lead to subpar work.

EXPECT YOUR COBBLER TO RESPECT YOUR SHOE CONSTRUCTION

Like shoemakers themselves, your cobbler should be protective of quality construction and not suggest a fix that cheapens it. If anything, your cobbler should add value to your shoes.

FIX A SQUEAK

Shoes that squeak—or yelp or squeal or whimper—are crazy-making for you and everyone around you. But there are some easy fixes. As you walk, listen for when the squeak happens, which can help determine the trouble spot based on what part of your foot is applying pressure on your shoe at that moment. Then consider a two-pronged approach. Noise often occurs based on friction, which can cause moisture. Try dropping in some baking soda, talcum powder, or even corn starch to alleviate that, targeting the trouble spot. Note: That may mean sprinkling a bit under the insole, if it's removable. If that doesn't help, it could be a sign that your shoe has air trapped somewhere in the sole itself, which means you may want to stop by your local cobbler for a quick fix.

Chapter Five

BRANDS
TO KNOW

Navigating the many options for the type of footwear that best suits your needs and personal taste is only part one of getting your footwear collection where it needs to be. You also need to choose which shoemaker makes the shoes you want to take out for a spin. Not to worry—we've compiled a list here of notable, trustworthy names in the world of shoes that can get you started out on the right foot.

ADIDAS

FOUNDER: Adi Dassler

ESTABLISHED: 1949, Herzogenaurach, Germany

KNOWN FOR: a classic assortment of iconic sneakers like the Stan Smith, Gazelle, Samba, and Superstar

....

One of the world's leading sneaker companies, Adidas offers performance footwear for playing sports in addition to the many timeless styles released under their Adidas Originals label.

ALDEN

FOUNDER: Charles H. Alden

ESTABLISHED: 1884, Massachusetts, USA

KNOWN FOR: handcrafted men's dress shoes made in the USA

....

Little has changed in the way Alden makes their shoes since the family-owned company first began manufacturing oxfords, derbies, and other timeless styles, a testament to the quality standards of each pair.

BASS

FOUNDER: George H. Bass

ESTABLISHED: 1876, Maine, USA

KNOWN FOR: all-American, preppy loafers called Weejuns

....

The signature G. H. Bass & Co. Weejuns have been worn in various iterations by everyone from JFK to Michael Jackson.

CHURCH'S

FOUNDER: Thomas Church

ESTABLISHED: 1873, Northampton, England

KNOWN FOR: a one-stop shop for oxfords, derbies, and other dress shoes designed to outlive passing trends

....

One of Church's most innovative styles—the Shanghai shoe, introduced in 1929—combines a monk-strap closure with a tassel and a rubber sole.

CLARKS

FOUNDERS: Cyrus and James Clark

ESTABLISHED: 1825, Street, England

KNOWN FOR: the unmistakable silhouettes of the Clarks moccasin-influenced Wallabees

....

Clarks offers a full assortment of desert boots, brogues, and loafers, but it's their Wallabees that remain their most instantly recognizable (and comfiest) style.

COMMON PROJECTS

FOUNDERS: Flavio Girolami and Prathan Poopat

ESTABLISHED: 2004, New York, USA

KNOWN FOR: their super-clean, ultra-luxe, office-approved Achilles sneakers

....

With an emphasis on Italian leather and minimal branding, Common Projects makes wearing sneakers where shoes were once required a feasible—and very stylish—option.

CONVERSE

FOUNDER: Marquis Mills Converse

ESTABLISHED: 1908, Massachusetts, USA

KNOWN FOR: the Chuck Taylor, a shoe that's remarkably simple and remarkably timeless

....

With little more than a canvas upper and a rubber sole, Converse Chuck Taylors are inexpensive and eternal, offering one of the best returns on investment in footwear in terms of versatility and no-brainer status.

DR. MARTENS

FOUNDER: Bill Griggs

ESTABLISHED: 1959, Northamptonshire, England

KNOWN FOR: the eight-holed 1460 boot and its many spinoffs, all with a trademark, bouncy, Airwair sole

....

Initially the brainchild of a German doctor, Dr. Martens gained worldwide notoriety when the Griggs family used their shoemaking know-how to refine and market boots that have become synonymous with youth in revolt.

EDWARD GREEN

FOUNDER: Edward Green

ESTABLISHED: 1890, Northampton, England

KNOWN FOR: traditional leather dress shoes fit for royalty and other men of discerning tastes

··················

Ernest Hemingway and the Duke of Windsor can't both be wrong; Edward Green footwear is the go-to brand for anyone who appreciates luxury, craftsmanship, and an unerring eye for detail.

FERRAGAMO

FOUNDER: Salvatore Ferragamo

ESTABLISHED: 1927, Florence, Italy

KNOWN FOR: embodying Italian leather expertise with a luxurious take on classic dress shoes

·················

Although leather shoes have been at the center of the company's men's output for decades, Ferragamo makes a strong case for coming to them for other needs, from ties and belts to wallets and cologne.

FLORSHEIM

FOUNDER: Milton S. Florsheim

ESTABLISHED: 1892, Chicago, USA

KNOWN FOR: a breadth of footwear options, spanning from reliable classics to trendy, affordable options

....

In the grand history of American shoemaking, Florsheim has continued to uphold standards of quality, even as the company has grown into an international business—meaning you won't have to spend as much for shoes that carry a torch for traditional footwear craftsmanship.

GUCCI

FOUNDER: Guccio Gucci

ESTABLISHED: 1921, Florence, Italy

KNOWN FOR: leather footwear of all varieties, but especially their enduring leather loafer

··················

Even all these years in, you're just as likely to spot a pair of Gucci's iconic loafers on the street as you are their more of-the-moment styles, such as flashy sneakers or boots adorned with the brand's interlocked double-G logo or classic horsebit hardware.

JOHN LOBB

FOUNDER: John Lobb

ESTABLISHED: 1866, London, England

KNOWN FOR: bespoke boots worn by British aristocracy and other well-heeled elite

....

With a product line that extends well beyond boots today, John Lobb delivers handmade footwear around the world and still maintains a healthy made-to-order business from Paris.

NIKE

FOUNDERS: Bill Bowerman and Phil Knight

ESTABLISHED: 1971, Oregon, USA

KNOWN FOR: an entire universe of performance-oriented and casual sneakers

....

As one of the most recognizable brands worldwide, Nike is perhaps the footwear company best suited to truly say they offer something for everyone in the market for a pair of sneakers, from innovative, ultralight running shoes to Air Jordans and classics like the retro Nike Cortez.

PRADA

FOUNDER: Mario Prada

ESTABLISHED: 1913, Milan, Italy

KNOWN FOR: classic footwear with an experimental, modern twist

....

Just as Prada clothing manages to look backward to tailoring tradition while pushing forward with innovative design flourishes, Prada footwear often subverts classic ideas with unexpected twists, such as chunky soles or sneaker-inspired details.

RED WING

FOUNDER: Charles H. Beckman

ESTABLISHED: 1905, Minnesota, USA

KNOWN FOR: hearty work boots refined enough for city life

....

Although they may also make oxfords and chukka boots, Red Wing is known for their long-standing status as a premier American bootmaker that emphasizes rugged style as much as durable craftsmanship.

SPERRY

FOUNDER: Paul A. Sperry

ESTABLISHED: 1935, Massachusetts, USA

KNOWN FOR: the Sperry Top-Sider boat shoe, an East Coast preppy stalwart

....

Sperry boat shoes are as synonymous with classic New England style as sailing, the upper-crust pastime whose devotees have relied on them for generations.

TIMBERLAND

FOUNDER: Nathan Swartz

ESTABLISHED: 1973, Massachusetts, USA

KNOWN FOR: the six-inch Timberland Yellow Boot, a quintessential American staple

....

Timberland boots meld the best of both worlds: durable, understated footwear that still manages to make a style statement, one of the reasons men of all stripes have kept them in heavy rotation for decades.

TOD'S

FOUNDER: Diego Della Valle

ESTABLISHED: 1978, Marche, Italy

KNOWN FOR: the Gommino, a high-end driving moccasin for the rich and those who aspire to be

....

There aren't many footwear options on the market more luxurious than a Tod's driving shoe, a slip-on that telegraphs a life of leisure as effectively as sports cars and a $10K wristwatch.

TRICKER'S

FOUNDER: Joseph Tricker

ESTABLISHED: 1829, Northampton, England

KNOWN FOR: country boots and shoes that don't look out of place on city streets

....

Originally catering to farmers and countryfolk across the United Kingdom, today Tricker's shoes are worn in both the barn and the boardroom.

WANT LES ESSENTIELS

FOUNDERS: Byron and Dexter Peart and Mark Wiltzer

ESTABLISHED: 2006, Montreal, Canada

KNOWN FOR: next-gen luxury footwear from the twins behind a wildly successful leather bag collection

....

When Want Les Essentiels introduced footwear nearly a decade after founding their leather accessories line, the brand established itself as a singular destination for sleek, well-executed, minimalist must-haves.

YUKETEN

FOUNDER: Yuki Matsuda

ESTABLISHED: 1989, California, USA

KNOWN FOR: artisanal footwear that ranges from mild to wild

....

One the one hand, Yuketen can give you classic styles like cordovan wing-tips and penny loafers; and on the other, snakeskin boat shoes and beaver fur guide boots. Pick your well-made poison.

Want to know more? Here are other people and places to help you become a modern footwear master.

Stores

·

THE ARMOURY
Hong Kong and New York
thearmoury.com

BARNEYS NEW YORK
locations across the USA
barneys.com

BODEGA
Boston and Los Angeles
bdgastore.com

CONCEPTS
Boston, New York, and Dubai
cncpts.com

LAPSTONE & HAMMER
Philadelphia
lapstoneandhammer.com

LEFFOT
New York
leffot.com

LEVEL SHOES
Dubai
levelshoes.com

LIBERTY
London
libertylondon.com

MATCHES
online
matchesfashion.com

MR PORTER
online
mrpoter.com

NORDSTROM
locations across the USA
nordstrom.com

SELFRIDGES
locations across the UK
selfridges.com

STADIUM GOODS
New York
stadiumgoods.com

Required Reading

ESQUIRE
esquire.com

GQ
gq.com

HIGHSNOBIETY
highsnobiety.com

THE JOURNAL
mrporter.com/journal

OFF DUTY DAILY
blogs.wsj.com/offduty

PUT THIS ON
putthison.com

THE SHOE SNOB
theshoesnobblog.com

SOLE COLLECTOR
solecollector.com

Instagram

@complexsneakers

@fabioattanasio

@menshoes

@menwithfootwear

@shortofshoes

@stevecalder

@streetetiquette

@theshoesnob_official

INDEX

STEVE DOOL is a writer and brand consultant. His work has appeared in the *New York Times*, *GQ*, *Esquire*, and *Vanity Fair*, and on CNN and Fashionista.com. He is the former Style Editor of *Complex Magazine*. Hailing from New York, Steve now resides in London. He's never met a loafer or a plain white sneaker he didn't like.

BILL BRAGG is an artist and illustrator who can usually be found drawing in his East London studio wearing a pair of beaten up Vans surrounded by pencil shavings (although he has been known to dust off a pair of brown oxford brogues for special occasions). He graduated from the Royal College of Art in 2005 and is a co-founder of the art collective and magazine *LE GUN*. He won the V&A Editorial Illustration Award in 2016 and his illustrations regularly appear in *The Guardian*, the *New York Times*, and *The New Yorker*.

TOBATRON is an illustrator born and raised in London. He is a regular contributor to publications such as *The Guardian*, *The Times*, *Esquire*, and *The Independent*. In 2017 he was awarded the World Illustration Award. Unfortunately he spent much of the 1990s wearing Reebok Classics or crap black loafers from Mr Byrite on Wood Green High Road.

Thank You

A world of thanks to everyone who had a hand (or foot) in making this book happen: Angelin Borsics, Ian Dingman, Danielle Deschenes, Robert Siek, Kevin Garcia, Ryan Jin, David Coggins, Dan Rookwood, Aaron Levine, Byron and Dexter Peart, Eric Jennings, Danny and the team at Mr Porter, Paul at PRC, David and Blake, Francesca at Zoi, my parents, and the wonderful staff at Mortimer House.

Library of Congress Cataloging-in-Publication Data is available.

ISBN 978-0-451-49804-5
Ebook ISBN 978-0-451-49805-2

Printed in China

Written by STEVE DOOL
Illustrations by BILL BRAGG
and TOBATRON
Book and cover design by
IAN DINGMAN

10 9 8 7 6 5 4 3 2 1

First Edition

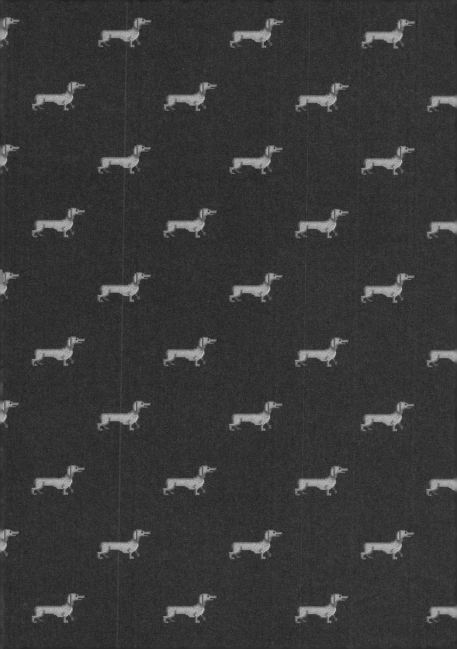

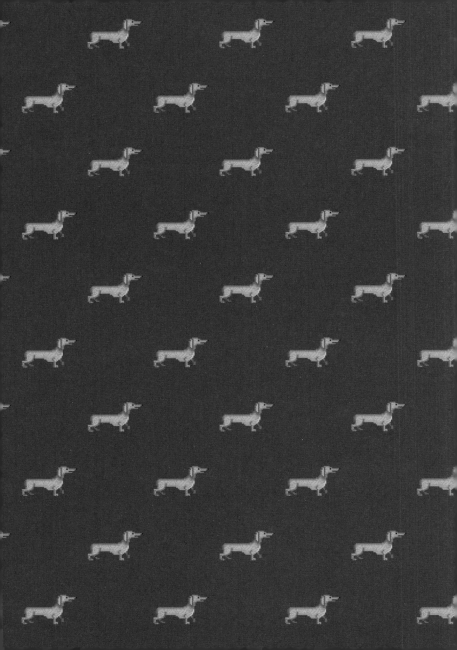